VIETNAM MADE ME WHO I AM

poems by

Karol Nielsen

Finishing Line Press
Georgetown, Kentucky

VIETNAM MADE ME WHO I AM

For my father

Copyright © 2020 by Karol Nielsen
ISBN 978-1-64662-340-2 First Edition
All rights reserved under International and Pan-American Copyright Conventions. No part of this book may be reproduced in any manner whatsoever without written permission from the publisher, except in the case of brief quotations embodied in critical articles and reviews.

ACKNOWLEDGMENTS

I'd like to thank the editors of Finishing Line Press, Leah Maines and Christen Kincaid, for publishing my chapbook. I'd like to thank the editors for publishing the following:

Columbia College Literary Review ~ "The Bear" and "Scuba Lesson on the Great Barrier Reef"
Abstract ~ "Spring"
Woodstock Poetry Society ~ "Neighbors" and "Poetry Is Dead"
The Moment: Wild, Poignant, Life-changing Stories from 125 Writers and Artists Famous & Obscure (Harper Perennial, 2012) ~ "Vietnam, Revisited" and "Vietnam Made Me Who I Am"
Used Furniture Review ~ "Bloodhound Eyes," "Faces of War," "Inferno," and "Life Sentence"
RiverSedge ~ "If Only I Sleep"
One Sentence Poems ~ "Hot Pink Dress"

I am grateful to Anton Yakovlev and Claudia Serea for writing beautiful blurbs for this chapbook; my sister, Cynthia Nielsen, for shooting my author photos; and my parents, Alan and Linda Nielsen, who are wonderful champions of my writing.

Publisher: Leah Huete de Maines
Editor: Christen Kincaid
Cover Art: Linda Nielsen
Author Photo: Cynthia Nielsen
Cover Design: Elizabeth Maines McCleavy

Order online: www.finishinglinepress.com
also available on amazon.com

Author inquiries and mail orders:
Finishing Line Press
P. O. Box 1626
Georgetown, Kentucky 40324
U. S. A.

Table of Contents

The Bear 1

Scuba Lesson on the Great Barrier Reef 2

Spring 3

Neighbors 4

Chere 5

Poetry Is Dead 6

Faces of War 7

Vietnam Made Me Who I Am 8

Vietnam, Revisited 9

Wilson 10

Bloodhound Eyes 11

Life Sentence 12

Inferno 13

Work 14

A Poem Doesn't Do Everything for You 15

If Only I Sleep 16

Hot Pink Dress 17

THE BEAR

The mountain was mist, cool white mist in summer. The trail—red dirt, rocks, gravel. My white running shoes became light orange, then rust. Halfway I heard a commotion. A black bear in the woods, rushing up the steep slope, deep into the green hills. I began to clap, in the white mist, and sing and chant. Like a spoken word artist, a marching band of one. I had no bear bell or whistle or spray. But I had hands and a voice. Noise, a warning that I was on the way up. Still.

I was alone that day, besides the bear. I marked the spot by a weathered milk gray telephone pole and went on. First the hotel ruins, like a bombed-out city hotel, abandoned on the mountain. Unfinished. A white elephant full of broken glass and weeds. No trash or graffiti or cigarette butts. Overgrown wild ruins, like ancient ruins in the Andes or Mexico or Mesopotamia.

I took a photo of the smaller ruin, a rectangular grid of empty panes, an imaginary window open to the inside. Outside. Green, so green. Leaves and brush. Grass and weeds. Moss and lichen, the color of copper rust on boulders sliced like loaves of bread. And lily pads in the water bath where tadpoles swam, where horse flies and mosquitoes and butterflies swooped and hovered and flew away.

SCUBA LESSON ON THE GREAT BARRIER REEF

Adam points to the clam,
encourages me to touch it
with a slow-motion nod,
extends a hand and sweeps
his palm across the lip.
Its undulating shell clamps
together like a bear trap.

This is not like shells on
the Long Island Sound,
so small I cup them
in my fist. This clam is
big as a bean bag chair,
velvet insides speckled
with lemon polka dots.

I am suspended. My breath
lumbers through rubber,
ears pop after I pinch my
nose, blow. Adam crosses
his arms over his chest,
floats, waits for me,
gives a slow blink.

My timid hand reaches
for the monstrous clam,
swipes its mossy lining,
and snatches away before
the shell snaps shut.
I rub my fingers together,
caressing oily residue.

SPRING

Spring is a tomboy all done up,
an amazon and a unicorn intertwined,
the reward after winter's test,
a fragile beauty in the end.

NEIGHBORS

I thought of his toenails,
metallic blue, and his sandals,
like a hippie, Birkenstock style,
and his jeans and military jacket,
olive with medals on the chest.
He had a beard and slim, slight frame
and looked as fierce as a warlord
as he stood outside the smoke shop
on the staid Upper East Side
while stuffy neighbors passed by.
Did he look at me the way
I used to look at them?

CHERE

I can see Chere, hip Chere,
with thick, long brown hair,
t-shirts and faded Levi's—
grunge cool before
Starbuck's set up
its first coffee shop.
Chere had it down.
Painter, sculptor, veteran
of St. Mark's Place;
her window overlooking
three decades of counter-
culture: hardcore piercings,
tattoos, studded leather,
fluorescent Mohawks—
hipsters, Goths, punks.
I once asked her about failure,
how to handle it. I was so sensitive
then. She said in the beginning,
when she sent slides to galleries
and they all said no, she would hide
under the covers for a week;
it was a waste, she said.

POETRY IS DEAD

Poetry is like my orchid.
Dead, near dead
from neglect
and hopelessness,
and in that barren soil,
buds come,
small bursts of color,
then full, fat blooms.

FACES OF WAR

The woman with red hair,
Army green shorts, wore
a black t-shirt that said,
Bush hates me. I wondered
how I was different. If.

The soldier on the news,
dead in Iraq, had a manly
jaw and arched eyebrows
like Cary Grant. I would
have liked to know him.

I lost the man I married
after Scuds landed heavy
on his heart; the sunshine
of youth, innocence, love
shrouded by midnight.

My father—family man,
business executive,
veteran of Vietnam—
told me that war is a waste,
but I had to learn it too.

VIETNAM MADE ME WHO I AM

I was six months old when my father left for Vietnam, as a first lieutenant in the 101st Airborne, the Screaming Eagles. My brother ran through the house like "Soupy-man," cape draped over his shoulders; "My daddy fly up in the air, my daddy fly up in the air!" I had no idea who my father was when he came home a year later, inching over the backrest of the car to sit between him and my chatty brother. I have no memory of this. I was too little then, but it is it ingrained in me like other memories of my father and his tour in Vietnam. These are collective memories, family memories, the quiet truths of war born by all of us, carried and curated as if our own. Then it was Vietnam, now it is Afghanistan, but war is all the same. When I saw a *New York Times* photo essay about one battalion's deployment to Afghanistan, I was moved by a sad man holding his baby, hugging his wife. As I looked at this man cradling his child, I thought of how my life changed as an infant, how those first six months of innocence were cut short, how Vietnam made me who I am.

VIETNAM, REVISITED

My father used to look at the stars
and think of me, my brother,
my mother. In short shorts.

In Vietnam, my father "saw some shit."
In the Central Highlands, along the central coast,
by the Cambodian border. I was a baby then.

I have no memory of an innocent time,
before I carried his war stories
in my head, like a movie I'd seen.

War makes no sense, my father always said.
We watch the *NewsHour* together, to honor the dead.
It ends quietly, like the silence of those who can no longer speak.

WILSON

My father choked up when he found Wilson's name among the dead on the Vietnam Veterans Memorial wall. Wilson was a hillbilly from the South who was going to be court martialed. My father's job was to straighten him out. Wilson was always joking around and he and my father became friends. When my mother sent popcorn to my father, he shared it with Wilson. Eventually, Wilson began to report to a new commanding officer in the artillery battery. He took pity on his men one night and didn't make them dig in. Wilson slept in the fire direction tent with all the maps laid out. When the North Vietnamese Army ambushed the battery before dawn, my father rolled off of his cot and rushed to one of the big guns. He ordered an anti-personnel round of fleshettes and repelled the attack. When it was over, he found Wilson lying in the fire direction tent. He told him to hang on, but he realized later that Wilson was probably already dead. My father won the Bronze Star for valor in battle. He said he wasn't trying to be a hero; he was just doing his job.

BLOODHOUND EYES

Audrey is dead. It was unexpected; she was
30, so young. I sat beside her in the youth
symphony—first violin, fourth chair,
behind her brother, Ben. We played Bach,
Beethoven, Mozart, Liszt—chins pressed
into violin rests, our horsehair bows swept
strings together.

Audrey was big as a linebacker, gawky as
a preteen, as spare of words and visible
emotion as a Buckingham guard. She had a
head full of feral hair, a football face, and
bloodhound eyes—large, droopy, sad,
as if she always knew her life would
end too soon.

LIFE SENTENCE

Maria Elena miscarried her child
after many months inside.
I lost my best friend —
a car accident, crushed lungs.
Josh lost his to suicide—
a bottle of pills, I think.

Rick found his father hanging
from a rope in the basement;
Martha watched her mother drinking,
slit her wrists; Genevieve remembers
hers bleeding in the bathtub, dead;
grown ups told her it wasn't true.

I wrote about a divorced woman,
a gun to her head in Penn Station;
and a pretty college student—raped,
shot, stuffed in the trunk of her car.
I bear these stories like a life sentence,
their grief indelible, like a prison tattoo.

INFERNO

You think because
you are older,
know better—
fire burns, but
life is an inferno,
and we must
nurse charred flesh,
cinders of soul,
or else we are
consumed, whole.

WORK

I write letters for specialty occupation visa applicants
in the name of professors of computer science, engineering,
chemistry, biology, finance, accounting, marketing, fashion design,
graphic design, food science, law. I am a ghost writer, using templates
created by other writers, shaping and adapting them to the particulars
of the case. The paycheck comes direct deposit every two weeks,
and already, in just six months, I have saved thousands. I never saved
during my long years as a journalist, working under the constant
pressure to keep sources from complaining about my work despite its
accuracy. I left journalism to become a writing teacher and editor but
it was never enough. I rarely traveled, too poor most of the time, but I
wrote and wrote. Now I struggle to say something poetic on my lunch
hour. It goes too fast.

A POEM DOESN'T DO EVERYTHING FOR YOU

Morning sunshine stretched a long shadow of my legs across the sidewalk on my way to work near the New York Public Library. I stopped, transfixed by the lines by my feet. "A poem doesn't do everything for you," wrote Gwendolyn Brooks. Her words fed my hunger for inspiration like a starving beggar. I wanted to answer her wisdom with a poem.

IF ONLY I SLEEP

Robin sent me that e-mail again, a questionnaire for friends. It asks, What's the worst feeling you can imagine? Robin said failure. I said fatigue, even though I used to think that divorce was the worst. Divorce isn't a feeling, but it should be, indicated by black circles under eyes, compulsive smoking, and deep fear that you'll be stuck forever with a low-level pain that makes crying come so easily.

I learned that love is resilient, but I'm never so sure I'll survive too little sleep: it abbreviates my patience, makes me forgetful and rude, and if I'm not careful, flat-out cruel. On those days of sleepy gloom I have visions of laborers toiling away for a morsel of bread, stuck in a filthy factory, industrial dread. That's my life, I think. Then I wake up laughing. Of course I can go on if only I sleep.

HOT PINK DRESS

I don't know how to hide
my underside, so I wear it
like a hot pink dress.

Karol Nielsen is the author of the memoirs *Walking A & P: A Vietnam War Memoir* (Mascot Books, 2018) and *Black Elephants* (Bison Books, 2011) and the poetry chapbook *This Woman I Thought I'd Be* (Finishing Line Press, 2012). *Black Elephants* was selected as a New and Noteworthy Book by *Poets & Writers* in 2011 and shortlisted for the William Saroyan International Prize for Writing in nonfiction in 2012. Excerpts were honored as notable essays in *The Best American Essays* in 2010 and 2005. Her poetry collection was a finalist for the Colorado Prize for Poetry in 2007. Her work has appeared in the anthology, *The Moment: Wild, Poignant, Life-changing Stories from 125 Artists and Writers Famous & Obscure* (Harper Perennial, 2012) and many publications, including *Abstract, Columbia College Literary Review, Epiphany, Forward, Guernica, Lumina, North Dakota Quarterly, Old Red Kimono, Permafrost, RiverSedge, Smith, Used Furniture Review,* and *Women's Voices for Change*. As a journalist, she contributed to *Jane's Intelligence Review, New York Newsday*, the *Stamford Advocate*, and many others. She has taught creative nonfiction and memoir writing at New York Writers Workshop and New York University.

www.ingramcontent.com/pod-product-compliance
Lightning Source LLC
LaVergne TN
LVHW041526070426
835507LV00013B/1850